MW01180805

Azu's Dreams of Cambodia
Angkor
Published in 2004 by AZU Editions Ltd.
13/F, Silver Fortune Plaza
1 Wellington Street
Central
Hong Kong

Produced by ink it Group Co. Ltd.
111 SKV Building, 3/F
Soi Sansabai, Sukhumvit Soi 36
Klongton, Klongtoey
Bangkok 10110, Thailand
Tel: 66 (0) 2661 2893
Fax: 66 (0) 2661 6895
info@inkitgroup.com
www.inkitgroup.com

ISBN 988-98140-1-3

Printed in Thailand

For information about reproduction rights
to the photographs in this book, contact
ink it Group Co. Ltd.

AZU'S
DREAMS OF CAMBODIA™

Angkor

Photographed by Mark Standen
Text by John Hoskin

AZU

'Suddenly,
and as if by enchantment,

the traveller seems to be transported from
barbarism to civilization, from profound darkness
to light.'

   Perhaps we cannot capture the same rapt
wonder that Henri Mouhot experienced when he
'rediscovered' Angkor in the mid-19th century,
yet the fabled ruins of the ancient Khmer capital
remain such as to hold every traveller spellbound.

   Portuguese and Spanish adventurers, long
before Mouhot, had thought Angkor so grand

that it must have been built by Alexander the Great or the Romans, while local legend held that it was the work of the gods themselves. Today, the myths and mysteries of Angkor's origins have been mostly explained by painstakingly gathered historical facts. Yet the romance persists, and Angkor's sheer size, awesome beauty and stark isolation conspire to conjure a sense of pure amazement.

'Just the approach to Angkor Wat is on a grander scale than anything in the living world,' commented English writer Sacheverell Sitwell in the 1960s.

Angkor literally means 'city' and here, close to the shores of Cambodia's Great Lake, the Khmer kings built their successive capitals and ruled over the greatest empire Southeast Asia has ever

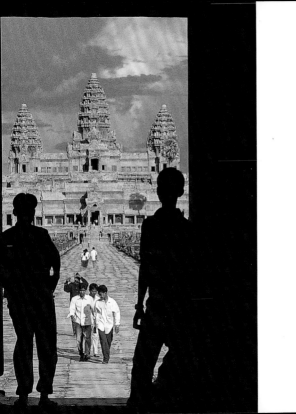

known. For more than 600 years, from the early 9th century to when it was finally abandoned in 1431 in the face of Thai onslaughts, Angkor was the heart of a rich and sophisticated civilization. In art and architecture its achievements equalled those of ancient Egypt and Greece.

Central to the civilization was the core belief in the god-king, originally an Indian concept that was adopted by Jayavarman II when he became Angkor's first king. As in India, a king was a god on earth, a divine representative of Indra, and a god's capital took the form of the universe in miniature. At its centre was the cosmic Mount Meru.

This cosmology was brilliantly expressed in Angkor's city planning, which centred on

the temple-mountain, which on the death of
a king became his funerary monument.

Largest and most perfectly constructed of
these architectural wonders is Angkor Wat, built
in the 12th century by King Suryavarman II.
A monument of unsurpassed beauty, grace
and symmetry, its huge rectangular stone
base encompasses three interior levels that
rise to a central core topped by five distinctive
towers, the tallest reaching 65 metres.

The proportions alone are dramatic, while epic
legends, war and courtly life unfold on the long
gallery walls, and celestial dancers and other

carved motifs enliven
labyrinthine chambers
and courtyards.

Angkor Wat is
but the most famous
of more than 70
major archaeological
monuments preserved

today, all with an
emotive power that
is as enchanting
as it is awe-inspiring.

The Bayon, a
fantasy in stone
with 54 towers each
carved with four
enigmatic faces of the Bodhisattva Avalokitesvara,
haunts and delights in equal measure.

The Baphuon expresses such extraordinary
self-assurance in its architecture to contrast
markedly with Preah Kahn, a tantalizing maze
of pavilions, halls and chapels.

Ta Prohm, intentionally left as it was found
in the 19th century, appears enveloped by
massive tree roots, tentacles that hold it in
the convoluted grip of monstrous nature,
distorting the stonework in a way that creates
a surreal effect, a Daliesque metaphor for the
persistence of memory.

Banteay Srei, isolated and so small that in comparison with Angkor Wat it is a minature model of a temple and yet, in the richness of its profusely carved red sandstone, it is an architectural jewel.

There is so much to explore, to marvel at and to ponder on the strange paths of history. During the 500 years after it was abandoned, Angkor witnessed bitter changes of fortune, reclaimed by nature so that it was virtually lost to the world, only later to suffer the ravages of war and man's greed. Against all odds it survives as a spectacular testament to the magnificent achievement of the ancient Khmer.

Cover: *Mosaic storm clouds passing over Angkor Wat.*

Pages 2–3: *The central core of Angkor Wat embodies a symbolic representation of the abode of the gods.*

Page 4: *Stone carving at Ta Prohm, a temple left untouched and still shrouded in vegetation.*

Page 6: *Raised on stilts, temporary villages dot the Great Lake during the fishing season.*

Page 7: *The towers of Angkor Wat loom in the cool-season mist of early morning.*

Page 8: *The central core of Angkor Wat is majestically approached via a long causeway.*

Page 9: *Thousands of Apsaras, celestial dancers, grace the walls of Angkor Wat.*

Page 10: *Seen from Phnom Bakheng, Angkor Wat rises above the jungle-covered plain.*

Page 11: *The enigmatic stone faces of the Bayon present a haunting sight.*

Page 12: *Angkor Wat's five central towers epitomize Khmer architectural genius.*

Pages 14–15: *Lightning forks across the night sky above the towers of Angkor Wat.*

Page 16: *A Buddhist monk walks through the cloisters of Angkor Wat.*

Pages 16–17: *Monks pass along the monumental western approach to Angkor Wat.*

Page 18: *In timeless fashion, children gather fruit in the shadow of Angkor Wat.*

Page 19: *Angkor Wat superbly mirrored in the pools flanking the western approach.*

Page 20: *Dancing for the gods, Apsaras are encountered at every turn at Angkor Wat.*

Pages 20–21: *One of two ruined libraries within Angkor Wat's outer enclosure.*

Pages 22–23: *The world's largest religious building, Angkor Wat is majestic and awesome.*

Page 24: *A devotee prays at the foot of a statue of Vishnu within Angkor Wat.*

Page 25: *A boy at Angkor Wat lends a human touch to the once-deserted ruins.*

Pages 26–27: *Angkor Wat's superbly executed bas-reliefs tell of gods and kings, of war and ritual.*

Page 28: *A carving on a stone pillar at Angkor Wat.*

Pages 28–29: *Shadows in the late afternoon accentuate Angkor Wat's labyrinthine architecture.*

Acknowledgements

The publisher would like to thank the following whose assistance has made this book possible:

Lap Tek, Yem Thoeun Navy and family, Hao Sotha and family, Meng Hieng, Soontorn Payabpruk, Wiripa Saeliew, Ramita Saisuwan and Keith Hardy.

Authors

Mark Standen is a British photographer who has lived in Thailand since 1989. His architectural training has influenced his photographic work, which largely focuses on relationships between people and architecture. He has photographed numerous books on travel and culture.

John Hoskin is an award-winning freelance travel writer who has been based in Thailand since 1979. He is the author of more than 20 books on travel, art and culture in Southeast Asia, and has had over 1,000 magazine articles published.